U.S. Department of Justice
Office of Justice Programs
National Institute of Justice

I0455244

NIJ

2007   2008   2009   2010   **2011**   2012

NIJ ANNUAL REPORT

U.S. Department of Justice
Office of Justice Programs
810 Seventh St. N.W.
Washington, DC 20531

Eric H. Holder, Jr.
Attorney General

Mary Lou Leary
Acting Assistant Attorney General

John H. Laub
Director, National Institute of Justice

This and other publications and products of
the National Institute of Justice can be
found at:

National Institute of Justice
http://www.nij.gov

Office of Justice Programs
Innovation • Partnerships • Safer
Neighborhoods
http://www.ojp.usdoj.gov

To the President, the Attorney General and the Congress:

It is my honor to transmit the National Institute of Justice's annual report on research, development and evaluation for fiscal year 2011, pursuant to Title I of the Omnibus Crime Control and Safe Streets Act of 1968 and Title II of the Homeland Security Act of 2002.

Respectfully submitted,

John H. Laub,
Director, National Institute of Justice

INTRODUCTION

The National Institute of Justice is the only federal agency devoted solely to bringing the benefits of scientific research and technology development to the nation's criminal justice system.

NIJ is the research, development and evaluation arm of the U.S. Department of Justice. It helps criminal justice professionals by conducting basic and applied research, assessing new technologies, promoting innovations and evaluating programs to learn what works and what does not work.

NIJ applies a rigorous scientific approach to its endeavors. Researchers harness the power of science to make the American justice system more effective, efficient and equitable. The Institute works closely with criminal justice professionals and researchers to establish its research priorities.

The following pages provide just a sampling of the most prominent work undertaken by NIJ. The Institute published research findings through the year. See the Research Report Digest at http://nij.gov/nij/publications/digest/welcome.htm

STRATEGIC CHALLENGES 2011

NIJ is committed to being a transforming force in the criminal justice field by meeting these challenges:

1. **FOSTERING SCIENCE-BASED CRIMINAL JUSTICE PRACTICE:** Supporting rigorous scientific research to ensure the safety of families, schools and communities.

2. **TRANSLATING KNOWLEDGE TO PRACTICE:** Disseminating rigorous scientific research to criminal justice professionals to advance what works best in crime prevention and reduction.

3. **ADVANCING TECHNOLOGY:** Building a more efficient, effective and fair criminal justice system.

4. **WORKING ACROSS DISCIPLINES:** Drawing on physical, forensic and social sciences to reduce crime and promote justice.

5. **ADOPTING A GLOBAL PERSPECTIVE:** Understanding crime rates and their social context at home and abroad.

TABLE OF CONTENTS

CHAPTER 1:

FOSTERING SCIENCE-BASED
CRIMINAL JUSTICE PRACTICE

Studies of Use of Force

NIJ published two reports about law enforcement officers' use of force, which include suggested guidelines for conducted energy device (CED) use. The *Study of Deaths Following Electro Muscular Disruption*, issued by a panel of medical experts, examined more than 300 instances where Americans died after being exposed to CEDs. CEDs are widely used in American law enforcement agencies, and in rare cases suspects have died after being exposed to the electricity. The panel found that the risk of death for the general population is less than 0.25 percent. The panel said officers who use CEDs should do so within accepted national guidelines and department policies. Police should avoid using CEDs against potentially at-risk groups such as children, the elderly and pregnant women. Because most deaths following CED use take place when a suspect experiences prolonged or repeated exposure to the electrical shocks, the panel recommended that officers avoid prolonged or repeated exposures.

The panel also recommended medical screening for suspects at the scene of the incident. In addition, it suggested that all deaths following CED use should be followed by an autopsy performed by a forensic pathologist. The risk of death due to only the direct effects of CED electrical shocks has not been demonstrated. Therefore, the panel cautioned against identifying CED use as the sole or primary reason for deaths cited on death certificates.

In a separate study, *Police Use of Force, Tasers and Other Less-Lethal Weapons,* researchers examined thousands of incidents where officers used various approaches to using force, including hands-on tactics, firearms, CEDs and pepper spray. In general, the study supported the use of less-lethal technologies such as CEDs and pepper spray because injuries to officers and suspects alike typically decline after law enforcement agencies start using such weapons. The researchers said that policies and training should ban CED use in the presence of flammable liquids or in circumstances where falling would pose unreasonable risks to the subjects, such as in elevated areas or next to traffic. Policies and training should also address the use of CEDs on suspects who are handcuffed or otherwise restrained and should either ban their use outright or limit them to clearly defined, aggravated circumstances.

> See http://www.nij.gov/topics/law-enforcement/officer-safety/use-of-force/welcome.htm.

School Violence Study

An NIJ-sponsored study found that school-level interventions reduced dating violence among middle school students by as much as 50 percent. The study used a multilevel, randomized control trial involving 2,500 sixth- and seventh-grade students at 30 New York City public schools to learn what prevented dating violence and sexual harassment. School-level interventions included using "respecting boundaries agreements," higher levels of faculty and security presence in areas within the school identified as "hot spots," and posters to increase awareness and encourage reporting of incidents to school officials. Classroom-level interventions delivered alone had no effect. These classroom

interventions included sessions that addressed the consequences for perpetrators of dating violence and sexual harassment, state laws and penalties, and discussion of sex roles and healthy relationships.

> See http://www.nij.gov/topics/crime/intimate-partner-violence/teen-dating-violence/welcome.htm.

Predicting Recidivism Among Sex Offenders

Risk assessments of sex offenders determine the likelihood that they will recidivate. Understanding a sex offender's likelihood of reoffending is critical in providing appropriate treatment and management. Services commensurate to an offender's risk level are most effective at increasing community safety and efficiently using tax dollars.

Researchers from the Vermont Department of Corrections examined risk assessment models that combined static (unchangeable aspects of an individual's history) and dynamic (potentially changeable) risk measures and found that combining these measures predicts sexual recidivism better than either type of measure alone. The study included 759 adult male sex offenders under correctional supervision in Vermont who were enrolled in community sex-offender treatment between 2001 and 2007. Offenders were assessed once using static measures based on their history and multiple times — shortly after their entry into community treatment and approximately every six months thereafter — using dynamic measures. Combining these measures through a logistic regression model consistently predicted recidivism and outperformed either instrument alone.

> See https://www.ncjrs.gov/pdffiles1/ nij/grants/236217.pdf.

Forensic Science Training and Educational Programs

Since 2007, NIJ has awarded a range of grants to develop and deliver no-cost training to state and local forensic science practitioners. The training courses cover many topics, ranging from digital evidence to fingerprints. The course delivery methods include traditional classrooms, hands-on laboratory-based instruction and computer- or Web-based instruction. More than 25,000 participants have received training for more than 245,000 total hours of instruction.

Below are four popular NIJ-funded training programs that were active in fiscal year 2011.

1. The New York City Office of Chief Medical Examiner initiated a Forensic Sciences Training Program in 2009. The program currently offers three practitioner-oriented courses: Medicolegal Investigation of Death, Forensic Specialties in Medicolegal Death Investigation and Bloodstain Pattern Analysis. Almost 350 participants have received this training. These courses give participants the ability to take what they learn and immediately put it into practice.

2. The goal of the Forensic Microscopy Program is to provide cost-effective training to forensic scientists in U.S. public crime laboratories in order to increase their ability to analyze trace evidence for law enforcement. The courses teach foundational as well as advanced and specialized microscopy skills in identifying glass, hair, fiber, paint and polymers and explosives. During the 2011 fiscal year, 126 students successfully completed the training in 16 of these courses.

3. The Center for Forensic Sciences within RTI International began producing and delivering Web-based continuing education courses for forensic science practitioners in the spring of 2008. The program originally targeted toxicology and controlled substances but has since grown to include courses in forensic DNA, anthropology, sexual assault investigations, expert testimony, laboratory management and professional responsibility. This program has reached more than 18,000 people in all 50 states and in more than 89 countries. RTI's website at www.forensicED.org receives upward of 10,000 visits monthly. More than 38,000 contact hours of training have been provided to forensic science practitioners; more than 10,000 contact hours were delivered in fiscal year 2011 alone. For some people, forensicED.org provides the only way to satisfy various training requirements.

4. The DNA Evidence Identification, Collection and Preservation for Law Enforcement course educated law enforcement personnel nationwide on advances in forensic science and the best practices for identifying, collecting and preserving DNA evidence. In fiscal year 2011, there were 32 courses hosted by law enforcement agencies across the country that helped 796 participants. This hands-on course is provided at strategically identified training

locations across the United States to heighten the impact of the training and to reduce costs. Law enforcement personnel have gained DNA evidence identification, collection and preservation skills from this course.

> See http://www.nij.gov/nij/training/ forensic.htm.

Help Seeking Among Victims of Intimate Partner Violence

Researchers examined intimate partner violence among Indians, Pakistanis and Filipinas who lived in the San Francisco Bay area. The sample included women between the ages of 18 and 60 who had experienced physical or sexual violence or stalking. Contrary to general perceptions that Asian women do not call the police, slightly more than half of these women had called the police at least once. However, they were less likely to take other measures, such as seeking legal assistance or contacting intimate partner violence programs for shelter or other services. Interviews revealed that the women hesitated for a variety of reasons. Some were simply unfamiliar with the criminal justice system, and others feared retaliation, wanted to keep the family intact, or had concerns about their immigration status. The researchers recommended providing interpretation services for Asian women who do not speak English and improving the cultural competency of criminal justice agencies in order to improve access to legal assistance and other services.

> See
> https://www.ncjrs.gov/pdffiles1/nij/ grants/236174.pdf.

Multisite Adult Drug Court Evaluation

What is the impact of adult drug courts on relapse, recidivism and other outcomes? For whom are they effective, and what are the costs and benefits? NIJ's Multisite Adult Drug Court Evaluation answered these questions with an unprecedented study of nearly 1800 drug court participants and comparison probationers from 29 jurisdictions across the United States. The study collected data from three waves of interviews, drug test results, administrative records on treatment and recidivism, court observations and interviews with staff and other stakeholders, and budget and other cost information.

The research, conducted by the Urban Institute, RTI and the Center for Court Innovation, found that adult drug courts significantly reduce drug use and criminal offending — both during and after program participation. Participants reported significantly less drug use (56% vs. 76%), were significantly less likely to test positive for drugs (29% vs. 46%) and reported significantly less criminal activity (40% vs. 53%). Participants also had fewer rearrests (52% vs. 62%), but the difference was not significant. Overall, the average net benefit of drug courts was estimated at $5,680 to $6,208 per participant.

> See http://www.nij.gov/nij/topics/ courts/drug-courts/madce.htm for more information on NIJ's Multisite Adult Drug Court Evaluation.
> Read the report by Shelli Rossman et al. at https://www.ncjrs.gov/App/ Publications/abstract.aspx?ID=25914.

CHAPTER 2:
TRANSLATING KNOWLEDGE TO
PRACTICE

Addressing DNA Backlogs

In response to the emerging backlog of samples and cases that needed DNA testing, Congress passed legislation in 2004 to fund programs that would reduce the backlog and improve the use of DNA technology in the criminal justice system. The legislation had several objectives, among them to increase the capacity of crime laboratories to process samples and to build up the nation's database of DNA profiles. By 2011, hundreds of millions of dollars had been spent to achieve these goals. Federal funding has had a significant impact on the backlog. Without the influx of federal support, the backlog problem would be much worse.

In November 2010, NIJ published *Making Sense of DNA Backlogs — Myths vs. Reality*, an analysis of progress on DNA testing from 2005 to 2009. According to grant reports sent to NIJ and surveys of crime laboratories, NIJ's DNA Backlog Reduction Program has helped crime laboratories nationwide to reduce backlogs by more than 211,000 cases so far. State and local DNA laboratories increased their capacity almost fourfold between 2005 and 2009. Without the federal funds to buy better equipment and hire more personnel, many laboratories would not have been able to increase their capacity much beyond the reported 2005 levels. Older cases have been processed, but even now the increasing demand for DNA processing has outstripped the capacity of the nation's crime laboratories. Funding provided for testing DNA database samples (from convicted offenders and arrestees) between 2005 and 2010 has resulted in testing more than 1.8 million samples. In 2011, the casework and database initiatives were combined into a single program.

NIJ's largest funding program is the DNA Backlog Reduction Program. The short-term goal is to reduce the backlog of unprocessed DNA samples. NIJ provides funds to participating crime laboratories so they can send samples to private laboratories for testing or conduct the testing in house. The long-term goal is to build the capacity of accredited public sector DNA laboratories. Laboratories use the funds to buy high-throughput instruments that handle multiple samples simultaneously, automated robotic systems and information management systems to process the data more efficiently and to confirm newer, more efficient laboratory procedures. Funds also can be used to hire more personnel, but most laboratories find that the greatest impact comes from a critical review of and changes in their processes and procedures.

> See http://www.nij.gov/topics/ forensics/lab-operations/evidence- backlogs/welcome.htm.

Attrition in Los Angeles Rape Cases

Researchers examined cases of rapes and attempted rapes that had been reported to the Los Angeles Police Department (LAPD) and the Los Angeles Sheriff's Department from 2005 to 2009. There were 5,031 cases reported to the LAPD during that period. Of these, 45.7 percent were cleared, 43.4 percent were open, and 10.9 percent were unfounded. Interviews were conducted with police officials, prosecutors and sexual assault victims to learn more about how and why various case dispositions take place.

In 2008, there were 81 cases unfounded by the LAPD in 2008. The researchers categorized 55 of these as false reports. Five cases were categorized as baseless, but not false. Ten cases were deemed not to be false reports; for eight of these cases the complainant recanted but there was evidence that it was motivated by fear, pressure, or a lack of interest in moving forward with the case, and for two of these cases the complainant did not recant and there was evidence a crime did occur. The remaining 11 cases were ambiguous, and the researchers felt they should have been investigated further before being cleared.

Complainant motivations for filing false reports fell into five overlapping categories. These included a desire to avoid trouble or a need for an alibi for consensual sex with someone other than a current partner, a desire to retaliate against a current or former partner, a need for attention or sympathy, and guilt or remorse as a result of consensual sexual activity. Many complainants in these cases had mental health issues that made it difficult for them to separate fact from fantasy.

The typical victim in the 2008 rape and attempted rape cases was a Latina in her mid-20s. A substantial number said they had been drinking or drunk at the time of the incident, but few reported illegal drug use. Nearly half suffered some type of collateral injury during the assault and said they had resisted physically and verbally. Most did not report the crime within an hour. Very few of the victims recanted, and only about one of every 10 said they did not want the suspect arrested. Most of the victims in the LAPD cases had been subdued with bodily force only, but more than a quarter had been subdued with a firearm, knife or other weapon.

The researchers found that some law enforcement officers appeared to adopt an "innocent until proven guilty" approach to these cases, whereas others had a "guilty until proven innocent" approach. Virtually all detectives made arrests in stranger rape cases; some made arrests based on the presence of probable cause regardless of whether the victim and suspect were acquainted; and some never made arrests in nonstranger cases, preferring to present the case to the district attorney's office for a pre-arrest filing evaluation.

Overall, there was substantial case attrition. Among the LAPD cases, one in nine was cleared by arrest, fewer than one in 10 resulted in the filing of charges, and only one in 13 resulted in a conviction. The researchers concluded that case attrition was based mainly on the decision to arrest or not; the vast majority of cases did not result in the arrest of a suspect.

> See http://www.nij.gov/topics/ forensics/lab-operations/evidence-backlogs/welcome.htm.

Cold Cases Training

NIJ has funded a series of cold case training sessions through the Virginia Center for Policing Innovation to help solve cases by using DNA evidence. Advances in DNA technology have significantly increased the successful analysis of aged or degraded biological evidence. As a result, police departments have solved serious crime cases, sometimes bringing people to

justice decades after the crime had been committed. NIJ awarded $4.3 million for cold cases involving violent crime.

> See https://www.ncjrs.gov/pdffiles1/ nij/grants/237582.pdf.

Postconviction DNA Funding

More than 270 Americans convicted of serious crimes and sentenced to prison have been freed because DNA testing confirmed their innocence. Recent advances in the technology of DNA testing have yielded definitive results in cases that might have been inconclusive in the past. Also, sometimes DNA testing was not available when people were convicted. NIJ's Postconviction DNA Program helps states to pay for reviewing cases, including finding and analyzing biological evidence. States that receive funding agree to comply with improved standards for storing biological evidence and to use accredited laboratories for DNA analysis. Some of the program's successes include these cases:

- Kerry Porter was released from a Kentucky prison in 2011 after serving 13 years for a murder he did not commit. Testing of a homemade firearm silencer found at the crime scene identified two DNA profiles, but neither belonged to Porter.

- In North Carolina, Kenneth Kagonyera and Robert Wilcoxson were freed and found innocent of any involvement in the 2000 murder of Walter Bowman. DNA from the crime scene implicated another person in the crime.

- In 2011, Johnny Pinchback was freed from a Texas prison after DNA testing showed he was innocent in a case involving two aggravated sexual assaults. Pinchback had been incarcerated for 26 years.

➢ See http://www.nij.gov/journals/262/ postconviction.htm.

CHAPTER 3:
ADVANCING TECHNOLOGY

Publication of "The Fingerprint Sourcebook"

In August 2011, NIJ released printed copies of "The Fingerprint Sourcebook," which was prepared with the International Association for Identification and meant to be the definitive resource on the science of fingerprint identification. NIJ released chapters online throughout 2011 as each section became available. The Sourcebook covers such topics as the anatomy and physiology of friction ridge skin (the uniquely ridged skin found on the palms and soles); perceptual, cognitive and psychological factors in expert identifications; and legal issues. The Sourcebook is now widely used in forensic training programs. It has quickly become one of the most popular publications in NIJ history. More than 1 million copies were downloaded from NIJ's website during the fiscal year.

➤ See http://www.nij.gov/pubs-sum/225320.htm.

Developing Standards and Testing Equipment

NIJ develops and publishes equipment standards that address the needs of law enforcement and corrections agencies. For example, NIJ developed standards for body armor, popularly known as bulletproof vests, which are credited with saving the lives of numerous law enforcement officers.

Standards ensure that equipment is safe, is reliable, and meets minimum established performance requirements. NIJ standards are voluntary; manufacturers are not required to use them. Developing a new standard entails a collaborative effort that begins with learning what people in the field need. Scientists and engineers help to develop the standard, which is then published in draft form. Law enforcement professionals and manufacturers have an opportunity to comment on the proposed standard before it is finalized. Accomplishments in 2011 include:

- NIJ published a new standard for suits that protect law enforcement officers from dangerous substances. The Protective Ensemble Standard for Law Enforcement covers suits that law enforcement officers can wear when entering areas that may have chemical, biological, radiological and nuclear (CBRN) materials. This standard considers the specific needs of law enforcement officers, such as the need for stealth and enough flexibility to use firearms and other equipment. The standard details performance requirements and specifies how to conduct testing to ensure that suits meet the standard.

- The Institute published a draft Vehicular Digital Multimedia Evidence Recording System Standard that covers equipment installed in police cars that is designed to capture digital evidence. The publication was made available for public comment.

- NIJ continued work to develop performance standards for equipment such as handcuffs and other restraints, holsters and electronic monitoring systems.

- The Institute launched a follow-on inspection and testing program to ensure that new lots of body armor previously found to meet NIJ performance standards

continue to meet the standards. The program includes manufacturing sites in the United States, Canada, Mexico and Colombia. The testing has included 126 models, including ballistic-resistant models and stab-resistant models. Of those, 76 have passed the tests.

- NIJ published 10 reports evaluating the performance of commercially available computer forensic tools. The National Institute of Standards and Technology conducted the testing.

  ➢ See http://nij.gov/topics/technology/ standards-testing/welcome.htm.

Development of New Forensic Software Tool

NIJ funded development of the P2P Marshal forensic software program. This program allows investigators to analyze peer-to-peer use on computers. Peer-to-peer file-sharing programs allow people to share data files, including text, audio and video. Although file-sharing programs have many legitimate uses, they can be used in illegal activities ranging from copyright infringement to distribution of child pornography. P2P Marshal is available free to U.S. law enforcement agencies.

  ➢ See http://www.nij.gov/nij/topics/ forensics/evidence/digital/training/ peer-to-peer.htm.

Closed-Circuit Television and Specialized Radar

NIJ funded development of a "smart" closed-circuit television system. The system uses an algorithm to assess physical movements that could be associated with illegal activities. For example, the system might detect movements that could involve a physical assault. The Schenectady Police Department in New York plans to test the new technology to learn how useful it is. Capping a long-term effort, the Institute also completed development of a prototype radar that can remotely find and track people inside a building. A company involved in this effort received a waiver from the Federal Communications Commission to use the radar for government purposes, a critical step in making the system available to law enforcement agencies. The waiver is necessary because radar systems have the potential to disrupt communications devices.

> ➤ See http://www.nij.gov/journals/258/through-the-wall-surveillance.html.

CHAPTER 4:
WORKING ACROSS DISCIPLINES

Keeping Officers Safe

Fatalities from traffic accidents are the leading cause of death for on-duty officers. Many of these deaths occur on the roadside as officers perform their duties. Firefighters and other first responders face similar hazards. NIJ has worked closely with the U.S. Fire Administration to find ways to alleviate the problem. Researchers examined factors such as reflective markings on emergency vehicles and the color of emergency lights that are most effective and least distracting for drivers. They found that chevron stripes are the most visible pattern and that blue is the easiest color to see both day and night.

Most police departments have traditionally placed their patrol officers on a 40-hour work-week in which personnel work five consecutive 8-hour shifts, followed by two days off. However, an increasing number of law enforcement agencies have moved to some variant of a compressed workweek. Some officers work four 10-hour shifts weekly or three 12-hour shifts (plus a time adjustment to make up the remaining 4 hours of the standard 40-hour work week). Few, if any, rigorous scientific studies examining the advantages and disadvantages of these work schedules for officers and their agencies have been completed, until now. In a study of police shifts, researchers found that officers got more sleep and police executives could improve morale and reduce overtime costs when officers worked 10-hour shifts. The 10-hour shifts did not adversely affect performance. The researchers used the most rigorous scientific technique available: a randomized controlled experiment. The Police Foundation conducted this NIJ-funded study.

A major study, published in the *Journal of the American Medical Association*, found that 40.4 percent of officers have at least one sleep disorder. Untreated sleep disorders may adversely affect the health and safety of officers. In other industries, such as airlines and trucking, lack of sleep is associated with increased risk of errors, injuries and vehicle crashes.

➢ See http://www.nij.gov/topics/ law-enforcement/officer-safety/ roadside-safety/welcome.htm.

➢ Visit http://jama.ama-assn.org/ content/306/23/2567.short.

Helping a Crime Laboratory

When the New Orleans Police Department lost its crime laboratory during Hurricane Katrina, it no longer had the ability to process DNA cases and eventually developed a backlog of hundreds of untested sexual assault kits. NIJ was able to leverage existing resources available through multiple grantees to address this issue. The Marshall University Forensic Science Center agreed to analyze the untested kits, and the Louisiana State Police Crime Laboratory allowed DNA analysts working for New Orleans to work in its facility and agreed to take charge of the untested kits. The National Association of District Attorneys and several other organizations also contributed to the effort.

The National Missing and Unidentified Persons System (NamUs)

NIJ developed NamUs to provide a centralized reporting system for missing person cases and cases of unidentified human remains. NIJ collaborated with medical examiners and coroners, law enforcement agencies, advocacy groups and the public, including families of those lost. The result of this collaboration is the computerized NamUs system, which anyone can use to search case records of missing persons and unidentified persons. In the past, these records were not easily accessible. In addition, the public was unable to search the available information or to help in these cases because access to the existing databases was restricted to law enforcement personnel.

Historically, families looking for loved ones had to call many agencies and look to several websites to find the information that now exists in one place. The recent development and launch of the NamUs website for NIJ is a groundbreaking step toward faster resolution of missing persons and unidentified persons cases, benefitting law enforcement and the community alike. At the end of 2011, there were 15,000 open cases in NamUs, and these numbers continue to increase every day. NamUs has helped to resolve 80 unidentified persons cases and 161 missing persons cases.

In October 2011, the NamUs program was awarded the August Vollmer Excellence in Forensic Science Award by the International Association of Chiefs of Police Forensic Science Committee. In September 2011, program manager Chuck Heurich and the NamUs team won the Samuel J. Heyman Service to America medal in the Justice and Law Enforcement category. The Service to America medal honors outstanding federal workers.

➢ See http://namus.gov.

Adolescent Sexual Assault Victims' Experiences

Researchers conducted interviews with 20 victims and examined records of 392 cases in two Midwestern communities. The study focused on Sexual Assault Nurse Examiner and Sexual Assault Response Team programs and the eventual outcome of cases in the criminal justice system. Victims with voluntary disclosure patterns were more likely to remain engaged with the legal system throughout the investigation process. The overall rate of guilty pleas or trial convictions in the cases was 40.3 percent for sexual assaults committed against adolescents 13-17 years old. Cases involving younger victims (ages 13-15) were significantly more likely to progress further through the system than assaults against older victims. Assaults against adolescents with documented developmental delays were eight times as likely to move further through the criminal justice system. An important finding was that teens often first disclosed a sexual assault to their peers. The path to the criminal justice system usually started with a voluntary disclosure to a peer and was followed by either a voluntary disclosure to a parent or an involuntary disclosure (to the parent through the teen confidant).

➢ See https://www.ncjrs.gov/pdffiles1/ nij/grants/234466.pdf.

CHAPTER 5:
ADOPTING A GLOBAL PERSPECTIVE

International Programs

In fiscal year 2011, NIJ remained active in the international arena. Its research investments focused on issues such as human trafficking and transnational organized crime. NIJ organized a major international conference that examined transnational organized crime in Africa and how it affects the United States. NIJ released two solicitations in these areas that resulted in four new projects. The Institute also hosted professionals and experts from numerous countries around the globe.

NIJ hosted a workshop on wrongful convictions that included experts from other countries. The group examined efforts to prevent wrongful convictions in various countries. The Institute also hosted an expert working group on indigent defense. Experts shared a variety of approaches to ensuring adequate defense representation for the poor.

- ➢ A report on the wrongful convictions workshop is at http://www.nij.gov/topics/courts/sentencing/international-perspective-on-wrongful-convictions.pdf.
- ➢ A report on the expert working group that examined indigent defense is at https://ncjrs.gov/pdffiles1/nij/236022.pdf.

CHAPTER 6:
HIGHLIGHTS OF NEW AWARDS
MADE IN 2011

Understanding the Impact of Child Abuse

NIJ is conducting a 30-year follow-up study of people who had been abused or neglected as children and a matched control group that had been part of an original NIJ-funded study. The study will examine whether adults who have documented histories of child abuse or neglect are more likely to be arrested for intimate partner violence or crimes against children. The study will also assess whether those who had been sexually abused as children are more likely to be arrested for sex crimes as adults. The original study had included 908 cases of substantiated cases of child abuse or neglect and a control group of 667 other children who were matched by race, sex and date of birth. In the follow-up study, researchers will examine arrest records for both groups. This effort, which is expected to take two years, may shed light on the long-term consequences of childhood maltreatment.

As part of the Attorney General's Defending Childhood Initiative, NIJ is evaluating demonstration programs designed to prevent or mitigate the impact of children's exposure to violence. Children exposed to violence are more likely to have aggression and conduct problems in the future. They are also at a higher risk of engaging in criminal behavior later in life. Eight sites, including two tribal areas, will participate in the program. They will focus on violence prevention and intervention efforts to treat the negative psychological effects that children experience when they are exposed to violence. Evaluation of the demonstration programs is critical for understanding how best to plan and implement strategies to reduce the number of children exposed to violence. Researchers at the Center for Court Innovation received a competitively awarded grant to conduct intensive process and impact evaluations of the programs.

Evaluation of Innovative Probation Program

NIJ worked with the Bureau of Justice Assistance to launch an effort to replicate and evaluate a promising, innovative probation program at four new sites. The four sites will replicate Hawaii's Opportunity Probation with Enforcement (HOPE) program. Hawaii's program identifies probationers at high risk of violating the terms of their community supervision and imposes frequent and random supervision conditions, such as drug testing and swift, certain jail stays for violations. The program also provides treatment when necessary. An NIJ-funded evaluation of Hawaii's drug-involved offenders in HOPE found that combining random drug tests and swift and certain sanctions for probation violations showed great promise. Compared with offenders who received conventional probation, after one year the HOPE probationers were 72 percent less likely to use drugs. They were also 55 percent less likely to be arrested for a new crime, 61 percent less likely to skip appointments with their probation officers, and 53 percent less likely to have their probation revoked.

NIJ and the Bureau of Justice Assistance are collaborating to test the Hawaii model at four new sites: Saline County, Ark.; Tarrant County, Texas; Essex County, Mass.; and Clackamas

County, Ore. All four sites have agreed to replicate the Hawaii model so evaluators can determine whether the effort can be successfully reproduced outside Hawaii. BJA is managing the demonstration sites. NIJ is managing the evaluations, which were awarded to RTI International through a competitive solicitation.

> ➤ See http://www.nij.gov/topics/corrections/community/drug-offenders/hawaii-hope.htm.

Expanded Prisoner Re-Entry Study

People who have criminal records often have trouble getting jobs. More than 80 percent of American employers conduct criminal background checks on job applicants. NIJ-sponsored research has produced empirical guidance for employers about when a former offender poses no more risk than any other demographically similar person. Researchers Al Blumstein and Kiminori Nakamura found that after enough time had passed, a former offender was no more likely to commit a crime than other people of the same age in the general population. A new research effort expands on this effort. The researchers hope to enhance the robustness of their original study by determining whether their findings are supported by data from other times and places.

> ➤ See http://www.nij.gov/topics/corrections/reentry/employment.htm.

Study of Kiosk Use for Probation and Parole

NIJ is sponsoring a study of the use of kiosk supervision for people on probation or parole. These arrangements allow people to check in at a kiosk, which may be located at a courthouse, instead of meeting with a probation or parole officer. Several states have adopted kiosk supervision for certain offenders. The study will assess the cost-effectiveness of the kiosks and examine how well they work. In addition, the study will include randomized controlled trials in three jurisdictions to compare kiosk-based and officer-based community supervision.

> ➢ See https://www.ncjrs.gov/pdffiles1/nij/sl000967.pdf.

Sexual Assault Kit Backlog Action Research Grants

Untested sexual assault kits (SAKs), also known as rape kits, are being discovered in police evidence rooms across the country. It is unknown how many unanalyzed SAKs there are nationwide. In April, NIJ awarded two grants for action research to examine the problem of untested SAKs. The grants are part of a project to identify the underlying reasons that SAK evidence is not tested and to develop practices that improve the criminal justice response to sexual assault. The sites selected are Houston, Texas, and Wayne County, Mich. Researchers are teaming up with representatives from the police department, crime laboratory, prosecutor's office and community-based victim service organizations to develop a strategy to tackle the problem of untested SAKs. A special

emphasis will be placed on how and when to notify victims when their SAK (which may be many years old) is going to be tested.

Partnerships Involving Researchers and Practitioners

In recent years, NIJ has awarded grants to teams of researchers and criminal justice practitioners who have proposed working jointly on various projects. These partnerships are uniquely fruitful because the participants complement one another, bringing their unique skills to bear on complex problems. Following are several examples of recently funded partnerships. One researcher will work as an "embedded criminologist" in the Pennsylvania Department of Corrections for 18 months to examine why the state's penal population is growing when America's overall prison population is starting to decline. The project will involve developing scientific policy options for lowering incarceration rates, with a particular emphasis on re-entry programs that help to reduce recidivism rates.

The Vera Institute for Justice will place researchers within the New York County District Attorney's Office to examine the complex relationship between prosecutorial decision-making and racial and ethnic justice. The project will measure the impact of a victim's or suspect's race or ethnicity on criminal cases. The Florida Department of Corrections and researchers from Florida State University will collaborate on several projects. They will evaluate the post-release impact of prison-based substance abuse treatment, assess work release programs, and evaluate post-release supervision.

Researchers from Southern Illinois University will work with St. Louis County, Mo., on a project related to hot spots policing. Crime mapping techniques allow police departments to identify crime hot spots, which can lead to lower crime rates as police focus on those areas. This work will also evaluate the effect of hot spots policing on citizens' attitudes related to police legitimacy.

Predictive Policing Pilot Programs

Predictive policing is an emerging field that applies advanced data analysis tools to reduce crime and improve public safety by predicting where trouble spots are most likely to surface. NIJ funded two pilot projects to test new approaches to predictive policing. The Chicago Police Department will evaluate the ability of modified pattern-matching software that is used for medical diagnostic purposes to predict crime patterns. The department will also evaluate software that quantifies and maps gang activity to predict emerging areas of gang conflict. The Shreveport Police Department in Louisiana will evaluate the "broken windows" theory of policing, which posits that small signs of disorder often predict where crime will emerge. The predictive model will use indicators such as complaints against juveniles, loud music, disorderly people, suspicious activity, loitering, disputes and prowlers. The efficacy of the model will be measured by its ability to reduce crimes such as shootings, robbery, burglary, auto break-ins, outside residential and business thefts and auto thefts.

> ➤ See http://www.nij.gov/journals/ 266/predictive.htm.

Appendix 1: Financial Data

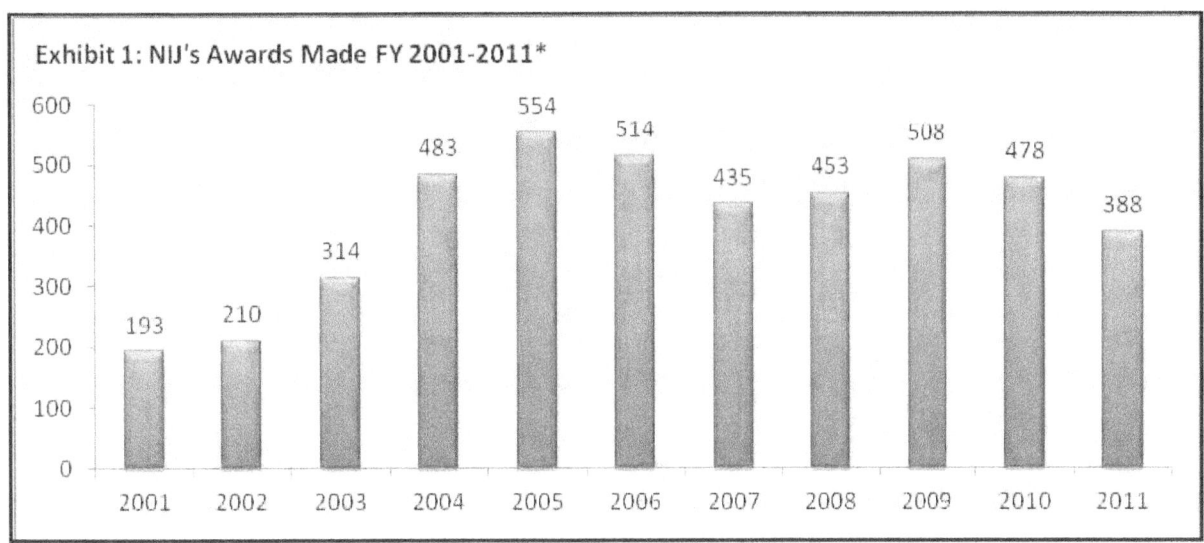

Exhibit 1: NIJ's Awards Made FY 2001-2011*

*For management purposes, the total awards made in 2011 include the DNA Initiative and Paul Coverdell Capacity awards as well as training awards: DNA Backlog Reduction (110 awards), Convicted Offender and/or Arrestee DNA Backlog Reduction Program (22 awards), Paul Coverdell (103 awards), Solving Cold Cases with DNA (27 awards), Postconviction (9 awards), and Training (23 awards).

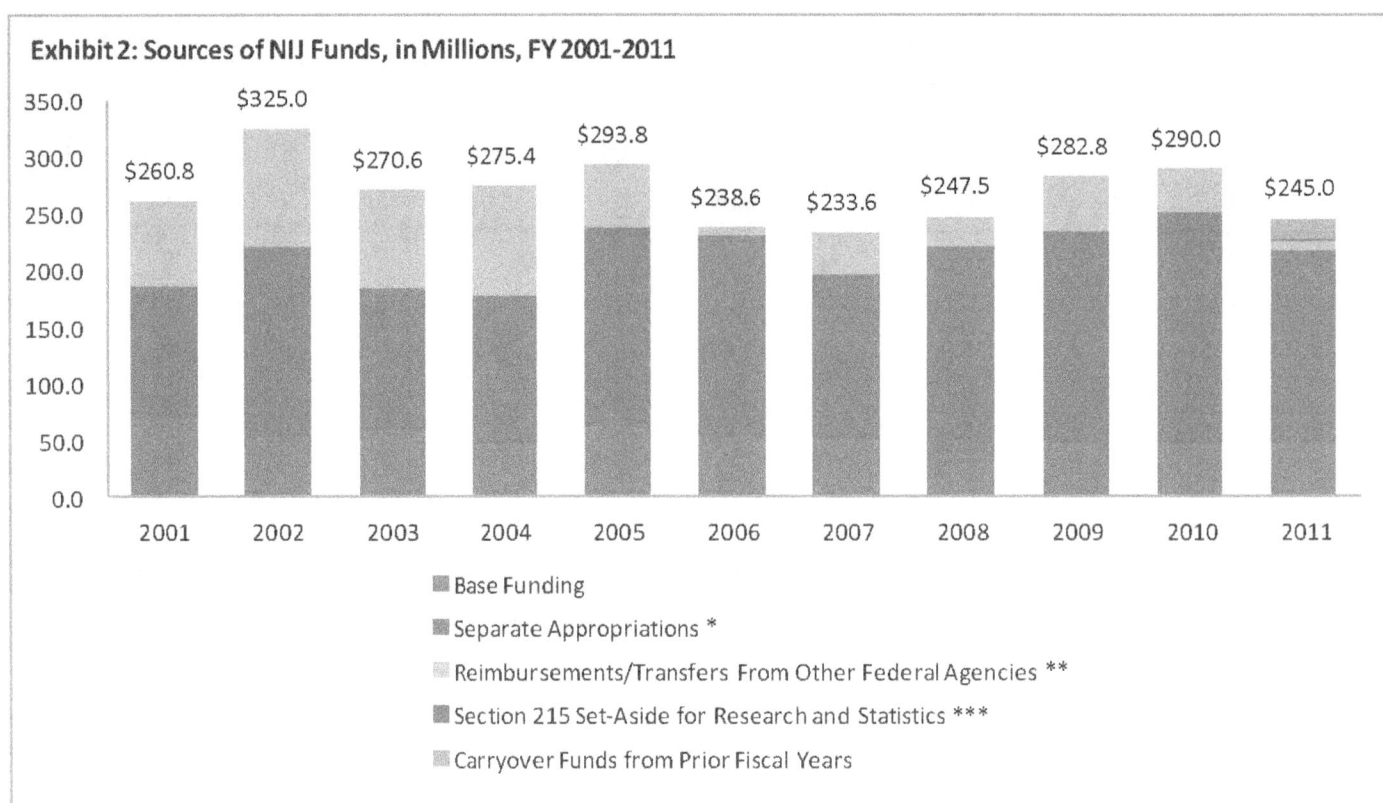

Exhibit 2: Sources of NIJ Funds, in Millions, FY 2001-2011

*In 2011, funds were appropriated by Public Law 111-118 as follows: (1) Under the State and Local Law Enforcement Assistance heading, $133.4 million for DNA-related and forensic programs and activities, $29 million for Paul Coverdell Forensic Science Improvement Grants, and $4.1 million for use in assisting units of local government to identify, select, develop, modernize and purchase new technologies for use by law enforcement. (2) Under the Violence Against Women heading, $3 million for research and evaluation of violence against women and related issues, and $0.8 million for analysis and research on violence against American Indian women.

**In 2011, reimbursements from other federal entities included the following: (1) $1.5 million to be transferred to the National Institute for Standards and Technology (NIST) for related research, testing and evaluation programs from the appropriation for the Bulletproof Vest Partnership (BVP) program administered by BJA. (2) $2.5 million from BJA for evaluation of the Honest Opportunity for Probation with Enforcement Demonstration Project (Project HOPE). (3) $3.6 million for various projects funded by other federal entities, including other OJP components.

***In 2011, Section 215 Set-Aside for Research and Statistics included the following funds: (1) $2.8 million made available to NIJ pursuant to Section 215 of Public Law 111-118 (AAG set-aside authority).

Exhibit 3: Allocation of NIJ Funds as a Percentage of Total Funding, FY 2011*

Category	Subcategory	Amount
Social Science	Evaluation	0.3%
	Research	10.9%
Science and Technology	Research and Development	5.3%
	Standards Development	0.4%
	Technology Assistance/Test and Evaluation	7.8%
Investigative and Forensic Science	Analysis and Capacity Enhancement**	50.6%
	Research and Development	6.6%
	Technology Assistance/Test and Evaluation	4.1%
	Training	2.1%
	National Missing and Unidentified Persons System (NamUs)	1.1%
Dissemination/Outreach/Program		5.3%
Reprogrammed per Congressional		2.0%
Carryover***		3.5%

*Total funding of $245.0 million consists of an NIJ "Base" appropriation of $48.0 million, plus separate FY 2011 appropriations that total $170.3 million, incoming reimbursements from other federal agencies that total $7.6 million, $2.8 million made available to NIJ pursuant to Section 215 of Public Law 111-118 (AAG set-aside authority), and "carryover" funds from prior fiscal years that total $16.3 million.

**Grants to improve and enhance crime laboratories (including funds for analyses/backlog reduction).

***Carryover funds are those that remained unobligated as of the end of the fiscal year. Depending on the provisions of future appropriations legislation, these funds may be subject to statutory rescission.

Exhibit 4: Funding for DNA-Related Forensic Programs and Activities, FY 2011

The National Institute of Justice received $133.4 million in FY 2011 appropriations for DNA-related and forensic programs and activities, which were used as follows:

DNA Analysis and Capacity Enhancement Program, and Other Forensic Activities	FY 2011 Funds, in Millions	Available Prior Year Carryover Funds, in Millions*
Forensic DNA Backlog Reduction	$88.7	
Solving Cold Cases with DNA	$4.4	
Forensic Science Training Development and Delivery	$3.5	$1.1
Research, Development and Evaluation	$13.5	$1.0
Strategic Approaches to Sexual Assault Kit (SAK) Evidence: An Action	$0.6	$0.9
National Missing and Unidentified Persons System (NamUs)	$2.6	
Forensic Science Technology Center of Excellence (FTCoE)	$4.5	
Federal Partnerships	$0.3	
Social Science Research in Forensics	$1.0	
Related Activities (including dissemination, outreach and program support for DNA- and forensics-related products)	$2.8	
Reprogrammed per Congressional Notice for Salaries and Expenses	$2.7	
*Carryover***	$0.5	
SUBTOTAL	**$125.1**	**$4.5**

Postconviction DNA Testing Program	FY 2011 Funds, in Millions	Available Prior Year Carryover Funds, in Millions*
Postconviction DNA Testing Assistance Program Grants	$4.0	$3.4
Reprogrammed per Congressional Notice for Salaries and Expenses	$0.1	
*Carryover***	$0.0	
SUBTOTAL	**$4.1**	**$3.4**

Sexual Assault Forensic Exam Program	FY 2011 Funds, in Millions	Available Prior Year Carryover Funds, in Millions*
Development, Delivery and Evaluation of Sexual Assault Forensic	$1.3	
Reprogrammed per Congressional Notice for Salaries and Expenses	$0.1	
*Carryover***	$2.7	$2.5
SUBTOTAL	**$4.1**	**$2.5**

TOTAL	**$133.3**	

*Awards made in FY 2011 with prior year carryover funds.

**Carryover funds are those that remained unobligated as of the end of the fiscal year. Depending on the provisions of future appropriations legislation, these funds may be subject to statutory rescission.

Appendix 2: The Nature of BJA-Funded Evaluation Research and Development Activities Under the Byrne Formula and Discretionary Grant Programs, 2011

Based on a full-year Continuing Resolution in FY 2011, $4,141,700* from the Byrne Justice Assistance Grant (JAG) funds was made available to NIJ for use in "... assisting units of local government to identify, select, develop, modernize, and purchase new technologies for use by law enforcement ...".

In coordination with BJA, which administers the JAG Program, NIJ used these funds in FY 2011 for the following purposes:

Competitively Awarded Grants

Wayne State University (2011-DE-BX-K003) — funds research to better characterize the types of sharp or edged weapons that are used in assaults on officers. This activity is part of an effort to develop improved methods to test stab-resistant body armor and help law enforcement and corrections agencies better identify and select armor to protect their officers.

Wayne State University (2011-DE-BX-K002) — funds research to characterize the injuries sustained by officers assaulted with knives and other types of cutting weapons. This effort will contribute to the design of stab-resistant body armor that better protects the officers wearing it.

Supplements to Competitively Awarded Grants

Center for Rural Development (CRD) (2009-IJ-CX-K019) — funds continuing provision of assistance to law enforcement agencies in identifying and acquiring surplus property through the Defense Department's excess property program. This is a collaborative effort between NIJ and the Law Enforcement Support Office of the Defense Logistics Agency. This work is being conducted through the National Law Enforcement and Corrections Technology Center (NLECTC) System's Small, Rural, Tribal, and Border Regional Center, which is hosted by CRD.

International Association of Chiefs of Police (2009-IJ-CX-K009) — funds continuing development of equipment performance standards for in-car ("dash") cameras, interview room video systems and automated license plate readers. These standards will help law enforcement agencies better identify and select technology to meet their needs.

Lockheed Martin (2010-MU-MU-K020) — funds an update of the NIJ performance standard for stab-resistant body armor and a continuance of the testing program that ensures the effectiveness of the body armor sold to law enforcement and corrections agencies. This work is being conducted by the NLECTC System's National Center, which is hosted by Lockheed Martin.

ManTech Corporation (2010-IJ-CX-K024) — funds the technical assessment of a "smart" video surveillance system to identify criminal activity in a crowd, as well as a radar that will enable SWAT teams to remotely locate and track individuals inside a building during hostage rescue operations. The video surveillance system was developed by General Electric Corporation under NIJ Recovery Act award 2009-SQ-B9-K013. The radar was developed for NIJ by Akela Inc. under NIJ Recovery Act award 2009-SQ-B9-K113. These assessments are being conducted by the NLECTC System's Sensor, Surveillance, and Biometric Technology Center of Excellence (COE), which is hosted by ManTech.

Sheriff's Association of Texas (2009-IJ-CX-K017) — funds continuing research to identify cost-effective options to meet the aviation needs of law enforcement agencies. The focus of this effort is on the needs of smaller, predominately rural law enforcement agencies that cannot afford traditional aviation solutions such as helicopters.

This activity includes support for NIJ's work with the FAA to develop a means for state and local agencies to use small, unmanned aircraft.

University of Denver (2010-IJ-CX-K003) — funds research to validate a method for testing offender tracking systems. This activity is part of a larger effort to develop a performance standard for the tracking systems used to monitor offenders under community supervision. This work is being conducted by the NLECTC System's Corrections COE, which is hosted by the University of Denver.

Agreements With Other Federal Agencies

Savannah River National Laboratory (SRNL) (2009-DE-R-107) — funds continued provision of technical assistance to NIJ in its efforts to develop equipment performance standards to help law enforcement agencies identify and select the equipment that best suits their needs.

Defense Technology Information Center (DTIC) (2011-MU-R-8316) — funds support the activities of the Interagency Board for Equipment Standardization and Interoperability (IAB). The IAB is sponsored by the Department of Homeland Security and is the voice of the responder community with respect to equipment standardization and interoperability issues. NIJ participates on the IAB to ensure that the technology needs of state, local and tribal law enforcement responders are addressed. Participation also allows NIJ to better coordinate its efforts to develop equipment performance standards with those of other federal agencies and standards development organizations. DTIC administers the support contract for the IAB.

National Institute of Standards and Technology (NIST) (2008-DN-R-121) — funds NIST's Standards Services Division to continue to support NIJ in its efforts to develop conformity assessment programs to better ensure the safety and effectiveness of the equipment sold to law enforcement agencies.

* Following reductions for Congressional Reprogramming to Salaries and Expenses and for the Section 215 Set-Aside for Research and Statistics (1% set-aside), NIJ received approximately $4 million for the activities detailed above.

Appendix 3: High-Priority Criminal Justice Technology Needs

NIJ's Office of Science and Technology serves as the national focal point for work on law enforcement technology. Title 6 of the Homeland Security Act requires the Office to report to Congress an assessment of the needs of federal, state and local law enforcement agencies with respect to technologies that support improved law enforcement.

Following are NIJ's high-priority criminal justice technology needs for 2011.

Protecting the Public

- Assured means to continuously and accurately monitor the location and status of offenders under supervision in the community.
- Safer, more cost-effective aerial surveillance solutions to identify, locate and track illicit activities and to locate missing persons, particularly for application with small and rural agencies. Solutions must consider regulatory requirements.
- "Intelligent" surveillance solutions providing automated incident awareness and warnings in public venues.
- Improved means to detect and respond to weapons concealed on an individual's body at a safe distance, including person-borne improvised explosive devices (IEDs).
- Improved, assured means to detect and effectively respond to vehicle-borne IEDs.
- Means to remotely locate and track cooperative and uncooperative individuals inside buildings in hostage rescue and search situations.
- Improved characterization of currently available, less-lethal devices and their health and safety effects, particularly on at-risk populations, leading to improved use-of-force protocols and to safer, more effective devices.
- New, safer, more effective less-lethal devices.
- Rapidly deployable, effective devices that can safely and remotely stop all types of vehicles under a variety of circumstances.
- Improved emergency-response solutions.

Some Relevant Efforts

NIJ is funding GE Global Research (New York) to develop a "smart" closed-circuit television (CCTV) system that will be able to potentially anticipate criminal activity in public spaces, as well as detect it. In a related effort, NIJ is funding Temple University (Pennsylvania) to quantify the size and geographic extent of the impact of CCTV systems on reducing crime. Despite their proliferation, there is little empirical evidence on the effectiveness of CCTV systems on crime reduction.

NIJ is funding the Providence Plan (Rhode Island) to develop a geospatial application to help corrections, public safety and social service agencies better supervise and assist returning prisoners. The Providence Plan will design a Web-based tool using "open source" software that will enable users to conduct specialized queries of the locations of released prisoners, map the results and overlay results with other spatially enabled data sets.

Ensuring Officer Safety
- Confirming and fixing an individual's identity under all circumstances in a timely manner.
- Assured means to continuously and accurately monitor the location and status of individuals and equipment.
- Improved solutions to assure communications under all circumstances.
- Improved means to detect, isolate, locate and defeat the use of unauthorized wireless communications devices in all operating environments, including but not limited to, correctional environments. Solutions must consider regulatory requirements.
- Improved, unobtrusive means to accurately detect a broad spectrum of contraband to preclude its introduction into correctional and other operational environments, such as courthouses.
- "Intelligent" surveillance solutions to monitor events in correctional and other operational environments and to identify and provide alerts on potentially dangerous situations prior to their occurring.
- Improved all-hazards protection for law enforcement and corrections officers.
- Proactive, targeted, location-based notification and distribution of alerts to officers.

Some Relevant Efforts

As part of its many related efforts to provide assured communications for criminal justice practitioners, NIJ has funded the Shared Spectrum Company (Virginia) to develop a spectrum management subsystem for cognitive radios. This subsystem will provide spectrum managers with flexible and adaptable tools to control a large number of cognitive radios. In addition, the subsystem facilitates the development and dissemination of a wide range of spectrum access and priority rules.

Confirming the Guilty and Protecting the Innocent
- Improved capability to expand the information that can be extracted from traditional types of forensic evidence and to quantify its evidentiary value.
- Improved capability to use and process digital evidence.
- Improved means to verify the veracity of interviews.
- Improved ability to effectively perform real-time, accurate identity checks across multiple jurisdictions and data systems.
- Fundamental research to improve understanding of the accuracy, reliability and measurement validity of the forensic science disciplines.

Some Relevant Efforts

In the field of forensics, NIJ-funded research led to the development of "mini-STRs" that can generate a DNA profile from aged, degraded or damaged samples such as skeletal remains. This has greatly expanded the power of DNA technology to identify the guilty, exonerate the innocent and identify the missing.

NIJ is also the largest funding source for research to improve the understanding of the accuracy, reliability and measurement validity of the forensic science disciplines. It has long funded this work in the area of impression evidence. NIJ is currently funding research at the University of California, Los Angeles, to examine how the visual complexity of a fingerprint and the examiner's perception, judgment and decision-making processes affect the error rates of latent fingerprint examination.

Improving the Efficiency of Justice

- "Intelligent" decision support systems.
- Improved information and data systems that link an individual's records and citations across various criminal justice databases from the time of entry into the criminal justice system.
- Secure Web applications (services) that facilitate effective cross-jurisdiction information and data sharing and exchange. Solutions must consider the Justice Reference Architecture.
- Immersive technologies to effectively train criminal justice practitioners, optimally at their stations.
- Devices providing multilingual speech translation capabilities for criminal justice applications.
- Reliable and widely applicable tools and technologies that allow faster, cheaper and less labor-intensive identification, collection, preservation and analysis of forensic evidence of all kinds and the reduction of existing case backlogs, including cold and missing person cases.

Some Relevant Efforts

NIJ funded the development, and funds the operation, of the National Missing and Unidentified Persons System (NamUs). NamUs is a clearinghouse for missing persons and unidentified decedent records. It is a free online system that can be searched by medical examiners, coroners, law enforcement officials and the general public to solve these cases. When a new missing person or unidentified decedent case is entered into NamUs, the system automatically performs cross-matching comparisons between the databases, searching for matches or similarities between cases.

NIJ is also funding development of the Forensic Information Data Exchange (FIDEX). FIDEX provides a bridge to connect the various databases used by law enforcement, crime laboratories and the courts to improve the efficiency with which cases are processed. Among its capabilities FIDEX enables the sharing of data between a police department records management system or evidence management system with a crime laboratory's information management system. It also enables the sharing of disposition information issued by local law enforcement and the prosecutors' offices with crime laboratories.

Enabling Informed Decision-Making

- Effective and instantaneous, user-transparent, operable and interoperable voice, data and multimedia communications under all circumstances.
- Improved spatial analysis tools and technologies.
- Affordable and open-source tools that can analyze data across databases and domains received through federated queries to create informed information-led intelligence.
- "Intelligent" automated solutions that can predict and deter potential criminal activity by correlating patterns of behavior and anomalies in that behavior from multiple data sources.
- Better solutions to the effective integration and management of sensor systems in law enforcement command and control systems.
- Automated case management and communications systems that can be used by officers and offenders to track compliance with conditions of release and prompt necessary action.
- Proactive, targeted, location-based notification and distribution of alerts to officers.

Some Relevant Efforts

NIJ has made a significant investment in development of cognitive and software-defined radio (SDR) and antenna technology for law enforcement application. It is, for example, funding the University of Texas at Dallas to implement a public safety SDR code in the Texas Instruments commercial Digital Radio Processor. It is also funding

Utah State University to develop an integrated, reconfigurable antenna for handheld SDRs using nanoelectromechanical systems (NEMS) technology. The proposed antenna will be compatible with multiband mode communications systems operating within the public safety radio bands of 150, 400, 700, 800 and 4900 MHz.

NIJ is the largest funding source for development of geospatial technologies for law enforcement application. It is funding Towson University (Maryland) to develop a new mathematical approach to geographic profiling. The software will be available at no cost to law enforcement agencies and researchers.

NIJ is funding the Research Triangle Institute (North Carolina) to create a software toolkit for processing and analyzing 911 calls for service to develop a clearer picture of criminal and homeland security threats. This effort will develop automated processes for identifying changes in small geographic areas, linking incidents across time and space, and associating seemingly unrelated 911 calls that are actually part of a larger sequence of events.